T0130054

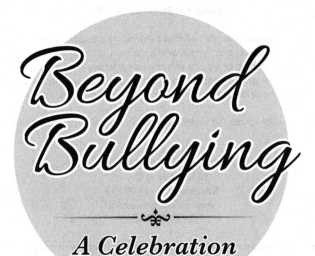

Beyond Bullying

A Celebration

Nancy Nikt

BALBOA.
PRESS

A DIVISION OF HAY HOUSE

Balboa Press books may be ordered through booksellers or by contacting:

Balboa Press
A Division of Hay House
1663 Liberty Drive
Bloomington, IN 47403
www.balboapress.com
1 (877) 407-4847

Because of the dynamic nature of the Internet, any web addresses or
links contained in this book may have changed since publication and may
no longer be valid. The views expressed in this work are solely those
of the author and do not necessarily reflect the views of the publisher,
and the publisher hereby disclaims any responsibility for them.

The author of this book does not dispense medical advice or prescribe
the use of any technique as a form of treatment for physical, emotional,
or medical problems without the advice of a physician, either directly
or indirectly. The intent of the author is only to offer information
of a general nature to help you in your quest for emotional and
spiritual well-being. In the event you use any of the information in
this book for yourself, which is your constitutional right, the author
and the publisher assume no responsibility for your actions.

Any people depicted in stock imagery provided by Thinkstock are
models, and such images are being used for illustrative purposes only.
Certain stock imagery © Thinkstock.

Print information available on the last page.

ISBN: 978-1-5043-5767-8 (sc)
ISBN: 978-1-5043-5769-2 (hc)
ISBN: 978-1-5043-5768-5 (e)

Library of Congress Control Number: 2016908728

Balboa Press rev. date: 11/07/2016

Dedication

This book is dedicated to my beautiful, intelligent, daughter Jasmine, who lives life her way. It is also a history for her because she remembers very little of her childhood.

Disclaimer

— ❧ —

In this book I relate observations of the behaviors and language of teachers, counselors and administrators of both private and public schools. The names of the individuals are not mentioned nor are the names of the schools. My intent is not to criticize or blame these individuals in any way. My intent is to demonstrate the result of the behaviors they exhibited in the life of one child. My hope is that those who read this will think before they accuse, before they judge, and before they make assumptions about anyone. As my father used to tell me "there but for the grace of God go I."

On a more positive note, I would also like to thank the five women who cared for my daughter when I went back to work after being able to be with her for only seven weeks. These women embraced her inner butterfly and she prospered; as one said to me "she is very well-adjusted for a two year old and she gets along well with adults and children." In third and fourth grade she was taught by two women who understood that she was never the one to start trouble, but that she would not back away from it either; and they supported her. In middle school, one of her teachers took notice of her studiousness and industry and asked Jasmine to grade papers for her. The group she went on a church trip to Munich with at the end of her first semester in high school accepted her and inspired her to pursue her interest in Scottish and Irish heritage and in learning the bagpipe. This gave her an outlet that got her through high school. She had two girl friends in high school that accepted her as she is. One young man in high school understood that Jasmine was under a lot of pressure because of the constant bullying and would tell the other students to "leave her alone, she has had enough." She attributes his intervention as the major reason she did not, as she said it "do a Columbine thing." There were two men who instructed her in how to play the bagpipe. I sincerely appreciate and thank these individuals for being a positive influence in her life.

I must also mention the help my older sister Sophie was in raising Jasmine. Sophie took care of Jasmine when I worked nights and also went to school. Jasmine learned a lot attending church meetings and helping out with my sister's volunteering events. One of the biggest things she learned was how to entertain herself; I never recall her saying she was bored. She also learned how to help others with her Aunt Sophie. Sophie also provided opportunities for her that I would not have been able to do on my own: trips, dance lessons, and piano lessons. I am very grateful that Sophie took a special interest in Jasmine when she was growing up.

Who Am I that You Should Listen to Me

—⚭—

I am one of five children born live out of nine pregnancies. My grandparents were all born in Poland and arrived in the United States in the first decade of the 1900s. My parents grew up during the depression. Neither of them went past the eighth grade in school. My childhood was a time of "children should be seen and not heard" and "spare the rod and spoil the child." My parents were under extreme financial stress and they made sure we learned the harsh lessons of life. However, we were also taught to "use our initiative," and be responsible for our actions and for our lives after reaching the age of 18, 17 for those of us born later in the year. I believe the phrase used was "you made your bed, now lie in it."

It was for the above reasons that, after leaving home at the age of 22, and moving 1000 miles away, I did not find it necessary or desirable to ask my parents' advice about anything and, heaven forbid, borrowing money from them was never an option. My siblings and I were working and paying rent for room and board immediately after leaving high school. Graduate on Saturday, pound the pavement looking for work the following Monday and woe be unto you if you came home without a job. From that time forward we were responsible for all our living expenses, car expenses and what have you.

I am still considered in my extended family as the adventurous one. You see, in my immigrant family no one left home until they were married, no matter what sex or age they were. It was unheard of to just up and leave home.

You are probably wondering how anyone raised in this way could do anything differently raising their own child. I kept the wheat and left the chaff behind. Actually, I learned how to raise my child because of the interaction I had with our animals and especially my horse. When I was five we moved thirty miles away from the city (Chicago) on a two and a half acre parcel of land with a small home that daddy promptly tore down to the foundation and built a two story house on. That's what they did in those days, just like the Amish do today; everyone in the family got together and raised the walls, at least the outside walls. After we moved in I remember being able to walk from the bathroom into the kitchen without using the door.

Daddy worked, and Ma and we kids (Daddy too when he came home from work) planted a half acre garden and raised chickens, geese, ducks and turkeys, not always at the same time. Of course we had the indispensable dog to scare away the raccoons and other wild animals and the house cat that took care of the numerous mice.

Ma said that I turned blue when I was born and it took the doctor a while to revive me, after that I was -- odd to say the least. These days autistic, at least high functioning, would probably be a more appropriate word. In January of 2013, my 65th year, my psychologist told me that my background and behaviors were consistent with being on the high functioning autistic spectrum. I felt good that I fit comfortably into some spectrum. For my part in my childhood I did everything I could to avoid being noticed because I was beaten and verbally abused for being too emotional and "doing everything wrong." I was in charge of taking care of the animals until I began working. Animals do not judge. I learned quickly that if I treated the animals kindly, took care of their necessities like water, food and clean cages and barns that they would also respond with kindness -- and eggs. Fowl are not likely to lay eggs and hatch them into little ones if they are under stress and upset all the time. I also learned that the dogs will come if you treat them kindly; they will run from you if you don't. Also I learned that farm dogs will not bite you if you respect the territory they are protecting.

Yes I had a horse. It was my dream. I only had him a year before I left home and him. He was what is called "green broke" which meant you could get on him and he wouldn't buck you off; however, he needed some work. His biggest drawback and my biggest lesson was his penchant for running away. Actually, when I brought him home he would not accept a bit; his mouth had been torn up because his previous owners had used a wicked bit on him to keep him from running away, which obviously didn't work. I borrowed a hackamore, a bitless bridle, from my neighbor across the street who raised and trained Quarter horses. My horse was a "grade thoroughbred" which meant he was mostly thoroughbred but his ancestry was actually unknown. Of course, he ran away immediately and I can't remember to this day how I stopped him. I asked my neighbor: how do you stop a horse with a hackamore that is determined to run away. She said grab the rein on one side about six inches from the bit, preferably the side the horse does not consider his strong side (the side opposite the one he starts off on), and put your hand on your hip. This has the effect of pulling the horse in a tight circle on the side he doesn't like to use. He will stop. Then you start again like usual and repeat if necessary. Eventually the horse will learn, and he did, that when he runs away he will be chasing his tail for a while until he stops. In people speak this is called natural consequences. Now you know because that is the technique I used with Jasmine.

Enough about me, this is Jasmine's story.

The Early Years

—— ❧ ——

I was 31 years old when Jasmine was born. I wanted her. Because she moved a lot in the womb the doctor told me she would be a boy. When resting I could see her little body making waves in my stomach and often I had to pry her little feet out from under my ribs. We walked a lot, she on the inside. I would recommend walking to any new mother. I walked even in the room before she was delivered while I was reading Irma Bombeck's book "If Life Is a Bowl of Cherries, What Am I Doing in the Pits?" For the most part I was totally alone during labor, she being born on Easter Sunday, even the doctor was the one on call not my regular doctor and the nurses came in once an hour or so and asked how I was doing. Even so, I had my Easter dinner, was dropped off at the hospital and four and a half hours later at 9:30 PM Jasmine was born. She was in good health and looked a lot like the half Cora Indian from Mexico that she is. We took a cab home around noon the next day and it was just the two of us.

I had what was called a Snuggly, a front pack-like baby carrier. I carried her in that while I did everything and talked to her nonstop (just like I did to the animals at home). I was okay talking with animals and babies under the age of three. I did not talk at all with older people unless I was expected to. I never talked baby talk; I talked to her like I would to any adult. The way I saw it Jasmine was my apprentice person and it was my responsibility to help her reach adulthood knowing everything she would need to know and having the confidence to do whatever she would want to do. I did not realize at the time how challenging this would get.

I do not want to bore you with a daily look at her life. I will just hit the highlights: the things she did that made me wonder.

I believe it was during her second or third monthly well baby visit, I was holding her upright on my lap while the doctor checked her ears. Then he took the ear piece off his flashlight and gave it to Jasmine to hold while he checked her eyes and mouth. After his check, he was talking with me holding the flashlight in his hand and Jasmine put the ear piece back on the flashlight. The doctor said he had never seen a baby that young do that.

For some odd reason she screamed and cried nonstop from 6 PM on until she fell asleep. The doctor said her nervous system was still developing and she would grow out of it, which she did -- at the age of six. Jasmine would cry and scream when CHiP (California Highway Patrol) would be on television. She definitely did not like seeing or hearing car crashes.

I worked full time after her first seven weeks, so I did not see her until the evening. I remember her crawling probably from about five months old. She said Mama when she was eight months old. From about nine months to eleven months, she would walk around the room holding onto the furniture. At eleven months she took off -- walking that is.

We lived on the third floor. The first time she left the apartment on her own two feet I told her to wait for me while I locked the door. She didn't wait and started down the stairs on her own. Of course she fell to the first landing and began screaming as loud as she could. She was okay; I picked her up and held her until she quieted down. When we started down the stairs again she would not hold my hand; she held onto the railing with two hands. I considered this event significant because she was too young to understand defiance; however, she knew what she wanted to do and intuitively knew how to do it safely when she was less than a year old. When people would tell me she was defiant when she was older, I would tell them she was born with an independent nature.

This is borne out by some of the other things she used to do in the 12 to 18 month range. When we were waiting for the bus I couldn't just hold her hand. I had to hang on to her with both arms while she would hit her head against my head wanting to be let down. At that point I couldn't trust her not to run into traffic.

Once when I was checking out at a store she bolted for the door and was half a block away before I caught up to her. Fortunately it was a long way to the street.

When she got a little older, closer to 18 months, she would walk ahead of me in the mall about 20 feet. She would duck into a store and I would look for the giggling clothes rack. She would always keep track of where I was and keep a constant distance. At this time she was sleeping alone in a twin bed. She was able to vault out of the crib successfully at about 11 months old.

This changed when she was 20 months old in January, 1981, after I told her father to leave because he was becoming more of a liability to the family than an asset. She would not sleep alone any more. She wanted to sleep with me and would feel around to make sure I was in the bed. This was challenging because to make ends meet I had to get up early to do typing jobs before work and work late on my sewing jobs after work and school. I would wait until she felt around for me, then get out of bed. I would take her with me and carry her on my shoulders to do my flyer delivery jobs on the weekend. In spite of this insecurity, she still got along well at the babysitter's.

She showed an early inclination to be afraid to learn new things; that if she did not know it already she did not think it could be learned. Our apartment had a swimming pool so I took Jasmine to mother and baby swimming classes to make sure she would be safe in the water. She was about 16 months old. She was crying and fearful in the water. We parents were supposed to move a little out in the water and have our child paddle to us. I was out about six feet and she slipped off the side of the pool. She immediately turned around and grabbed onto the side of the pool. After that she was more confident in the water. She actually received her trout certificate after taking swimming lessons when she was three.

Jasmine turned two years old in April, 1981. My brother got married on her birthday and we went to Illinois for the wedding. I had to wait with her outside the door to the church because I could not keep her from running up the aisle to "see Jesus." She was always attempting to escape from the crying room at church at home. Once she succeeded and was well on her way up the aisle. Fortunately, one of the ushers grabbed her for me. She did not try this again since an authority figure, beside mama, stopped her.

While in Illinois she went with an uncle for a ride in the car. He was amazed that she was able to carry on an adult conversation at the age of two. At the wedding reception, Jasmine's cousin Roxanne, who is eight months older than Jasmine, said Jasmine is going off on her own. I let her do this because it was an enclosed hall. She went around introducing herself to all of her relatives.

Roxanne's birthday is in August. My sister Sophie told me she was looking for a Hungry Hippo game that Roxanne wanted for her third birthday in a toy warehouse with walls full of games stacked on top of each other. Jasmine pointed out the Hungry Hippo game to her; only the words on the side of the box were showing. Another time she pointed out a Burger King to her Aunt based on the word King alone. She always wanted to be read to. She would grab a book, shove it at whoever was near, and say "read."

Portent of things to Come

———— ❧ ————

Jasmine started going to day care facilities when she was two and a half and potty trained. Actually she was going two days a week because I was working nights and attending school during the day and needed to sleep.

At first things went well. Then the person in charge of her told me she was behaving badly for a four year old. The day care center had a new staff member who thought Jasmine was four years old not two and a half. Her behavior was actually age appropriate. After the new staff member arrived, Jasmine was reluctant to go to the day care center. The staff member said she thought Jasmine was four because she was over three feet tall and spoke as well as a four year old. That was true.

When she would say "boo bate" for toothpaste and "jewwy" for jelly, I demonstrated and had her repeat the correct sound until she could say it correctly. She could even say her last name with a Spanish accent until one of her babysitters corrected her. As I said I talked to her constantly and she soon was able to carry on a pretty good conversation. One day Jasmine came home and told me that she "accidentally went into the boys' bathroom by mistake and that boys had a little hose to go to the bathroom" and she wanted one. I had to explain to her that only boys had those little hoses.

When Jasmine was three we moved from the apartment she knew to an almost identical apartment on the family side of the complex. My sister also moved in with us. Jasmine seemed to be much more uncomfortable with change since the time her father left. She began grinding her teeth at night after we moved. She was sure of herself and what she wanted though. She was in line to go down a slide and an older boy tried to cut in front of her. She didn't let him.

Jasmine only wanted one other child at her third birthday party, a boy at the day care that was five years old.

She was in a singing and dancing group when she was three. One little boy froze and was not able to do his solo, Jasmine grabbed the mike and sang it for him.

My sister Mona told me of an incident when Jasmine was three years old. Mona, my sister Sophie, my mother and Jasmine were at a store and Jasmine wanted to buy her own item at the store like the big girl she always was. They gave her the money to pay for her purchase. Jasmine gave the casher the money and the cashier gave her the change and the bag with her purchase. Jasmine politely said thank you and stood there. Then all of a sudden she said to the casher, "Hey! How about a you're welcome!"

By her fourth birthday party at the skating rink, everyone in her class came and she showed clear indications of being a natural leader at that time. All her fellow students liked her and looked up to her.

At that time she went to a new day care facility that had also had a prekindergarten. She got along well at the new facility until she was four years old. Halfway through the year the prekindergarten teacher told me Jasmine wasn't following directions; that she was circling answers instead of underlining them as instructed. Of course I asked the teacher if she had discussed this problem with Jasmine. She hadn't and wanted me to correct Jasmine's behavior. I discussed it with Jasmine as follows "Jasmine why did you circle the answers instead of underlining them as your teacher told you to?" Jasmine said "Oh I finished those pages a long time ago, before the teacher had the class do them." The teacher was amazed that Jasmine could understand the requirements and get the answers right without having the directions read to her. I told the teacher if she wanted the class, particularly Jasmine, to do the pages when she could give them directions that she should hand out the books before the class and not give them to the students at the beginning of the school year.

At Christmastime when she was four, I had to pick up an item at the Sears catalog counter. There was usually a wait and Jasmine was not good at waiting so I told her to stay in the Christmas decorations and toys next to the catalog department until I picked up my item. It took a very long time. When I came back to Christmas decorations and toys I did not see her. I began walking up the main aisle and saw her seated on the customer service counter. I was told by the attendant that she had come to her and said "my mama is lost."

The School Years - When it Begins

I have to preface this section with what I was experiencing with Jasmine at home at the time. My sister and I bought a townhome in September when Jasmine was four years old. We still took her to the prekindergarten class in the part of town we used to live in and she attended kindergarten in the private school where we went to church in our old neighborhood. In the day care in the summer before Kindergarten, close to our townhome, Jasmine learned to print her name and the entire class was taken to the library and all were given a library card. Jasmine still has the library card with her first hand printed signature.

Jasmine loved to be read to and when we went to the library would pick out lots of books she wanted read to her. I limited her to 15 books at a time. I knew that Jasmine was able to read, she had read words and phrases since the age of two. For some reason she did not believe she would be able to read a whole book. So I told her okay I will read a sentence and then you read a sentence, then I will read a sentence and so on. Before we got to the end of that book she realized she could read on her own and read the 15 books we had gotten from the library in a few days. Every two days we went to the library for 15 more books for her to read.

When summer was over Jasmine attended the private school attached to the church my sister and I attended at the time. I wanted her to go to the nearby public school since she did so well in the neighborhood day care. I was overruled by my older sister. She started in half day Kindergarten at the age of five. Since both my sister and I worked during the day, Jasmine went home with a stay-at-home Mom whose son was also in Kindergarten. The Mom was amazed that Jasmine insisted on taking a nap while everyone else was watching movies. I found out from Jasmine that she did not like the movies that were being watched and so opted to take a nap. She was always the independent thinker. Actually the movies they were watching were R rated. Jasmine did not see an R rated movie until she saw Schindler's List. I accompanied her at her request to see it.

School started in August and by October the school principal was calling to complain about Jasmine's behavior. The principal insisted that my daughter be seen by a mental health professional. I made an appointment for her at the HMO mental health department where I was insured through work. The therapist asked me what was her problem and I said I did not have problems with her at home and gave her the phone number of the Principal. I never did find out the content of that conversation. However, I was told by the therapist that my child's "problem" was too severe for her to be seen at the HMO mental health department and that there was no appeal that could be made in this regard.

I was working sixty hours a week and attending graduate school of business full time while this was going on. I felt my only option to help Jasmine was taken away. The principal told me she and the other teachers were having so much difficulty with Jasmine that they went to a behavioral counselor in the public school for assistance. They told the behavioral counselor that Jasmine's behavior was not appropriate for Kindergarten. The behavioral counselor asked them if they ever told Jasmine her behavior was not appropriate for Kindergarten. They hadn't. This apparently had never occurred to them. The majority of the children in the private school had been home with their mothers until they attended Kindergarten. Jasmine had caregivers since the age of seven weeks. She expected to be told what behaviors were appropriate in a new situation. When she knew what the rules were, she followed them without question. When she was not told upfront how to behave and what to expect, she would watch the other children for quite a while to see what they were doing and how they were behaving and only then would she try those behaviors.

I had an opportunity to witness this happening in her Kindergarten class. The parents were invited to come to the class for a celebration of some type. There were refreshments and the children's work was displayed. Jasmine was sitting in her seat observing the other children and saw that some of them were climbing on what looked to be a ladder to a loft. Jasmine observed for some time, and then she too started to climb on the ladder. Almost immediately the teacher admonished Jasmine, and only Jasmine, for this behavior. The other children had come down but their behavior in climbing on this ladder was never brought up by the teacher.

The teacher had segregated Jasmine in a corner in a desk by herself so that she was not in a position to distract the other children. The behavioral consultant told the teacher that social isolation was not a good way to handle their problems with Jasmine. I found out later that the principal was calling my daughter an "evil" child who did not know right from wrong.

I knew this to be inaccurate because at the age of two and a half Jasmine told her caregiver that another child in her care was attempting to injure a baby also in her care. To me that is very strong evidence that Jasmine was aware of right and wrong at a very young age. Of course my thoughts and my opinions were invalidated by the Principal because I was after all a single parent and how could I know.

The Kindergarten teacher was teaching her first year and Jasmine was beyond the scope of her knowledge, so the Principal was constantly intervening. I was told that Jasmine is asking many questions to deliberately aggravate the teacher. I told them Jasmine understands things at a different level than many children and she is just attempting to clarify her understanding.

Nevertheless Jasmine made it through Kindergarten and went on to first grade in the same school. More problems arose. I was told that I needed to correct Jasmine's behavior in the lunchroom; every day she would get into trouble for some reason or other. I asked the teacher if anyone had talked to Jasmine about it and of course no one had. I asked Jasmine in a very matter of fact way "why do you get in trouble in the lunchroom every day?" Jasmine very excitedly replied "they give out work papers for punishment and I love those." You can imagine how well that went over when I told the teachers their punishments were a reward to Jasmine.

I found a little humor in the time I was called and told by the teacher that Jasmine must be sick because she was not being her usual self.

When the entire school was engaged in an art project, I was told by the Principal that the detail in Jasmine's rendering was very advanced for a child her age.

The Principal wanted me to have Jasmine put on medication for hyperactivity. I did discuss this with her doctor; the same doctor she had since she was a baby. He asked me if she was able to pay attention to anything. I told him oh yes; when she was interested in something she was totally focused on learning as much as she could about it. The doctor wisely said Jasmine doesn't need medication. As the doctor told me when Jasmine cried every evening, he said people say things like he/she is such a good baby. He said a baby isn't bad or good; just more convenient or less convenient for their parents.

There were a few times at home when Jasmine was six and in the first grade that she surprised me. One evening she was watching a story on television originally written by Edgar Allen Poe, Murders on the Rue Morgue. I told her it was time for bed and she said the story isn't finished yet. I gave her the complete works of Edgar Allen Poe and told her to read it and find out the ending. The next morning I asked her how the story ended and she said the monkey did it. That was correct because in the story a woman was killed in a closed room on an upper floor by a large ape that came in through the window. To find this out, she had to read the story descriptions, select the right story and read it to the end. In the book the monkey is called an Orang-outang.

In April the year she was six, 1985, the Titanic was found at the bottom of the ocean and Jasmine saw it on the news. She told me "it sank on my birthday and I want to find out more about it." I told her the National Geographic had an article in the April, 1985, issue and gave it to her to read. From there she went on to acquire every book, video, and reference of any kind regarding the Titanic. She attended lectures on it and became a member of the Titanic Historical Society. Later on when she was 12-13 she volunteered for the Molly Brown House as a page to assist with tours and was called upon to give the account of the sinking of the Titanic to the guests.

When Jasmine was seven in the second grade she went to first Holy Communion. I was told before this event that I had to make Jasmine behave at the ceremony. The conversation I had with her went something like this. Jasmine on normal days in church it is possible to have some variation in your behavior, but today is not one of those days. Today is a very special holy day and it is very important to the nuns and teachers that everything happens perfectly today. So today would be a very good day to choose to be on your best behavior. Jasmine was an angel that day, folded hands, no squirming; no doing anything she was not told to do. She was an angel because she chose to be one that day.

Another teaching moment occurred around this time when Jasmine was in a ballet recital. She became angry and frustrated and refused to cooperate shortly before her group was to take the stage to perform. I told her I was going to leave to go into the audience and she needed to make a decision if she was going to participate or not. She came out with the rest of the children and performed well. She was in ballet from 1982 through 1987.

Many people, my father included, admonished me to make Jasmine behave and to punish her to control her behavior. I believed and still do that her independent nature was a good thing and that the best thing I could do for her was to teach her to control her own behavior; to teach her to make appropriate decisions.

It was important to me to not react negatively to her independent exuberant behavior. Her father was the same way when he was young. His father beat him for it and his mother left his father. Yet he was still considered a bad seed. He tried very hard to live up to that expectation.

I did not want that for my daughter. I chose to see her independent nature as a positive and acknowledged everything she did of a positive nature. There were several lessons she needed to learn, however. When she was very young she took candy from a store and we had left before I noticed it. I told her it was wrong to take things without paying and we went back to the store and returned the candy.

Jasmine was always independent. I always gave her choices and went over the possibilities of outcome of each. I would not call Jasmine bad or a bad seed. I thought this would absolve her from responsibility because her nature was responsible for her behavior not the choices she made. I taught Jasmine that she was always one hundred percent responsible for the choices she made and also one hundred percent responsible for the consequences of her choices.

I always told her whichever way she chose to behave she would have to be able to live with the consequences so she should choose wisely. Sometimes I would tell her she would not be able to go somewhere or not watch something on television if she did not do something I wanted her to do. She could very easily tell me "I could forego it" and she would choose to take the consequences.

In elementary school she was with some neighborhood children who egged one of the neighbor's townhomes. She did not do the egging; however, I told her she was as responsible for it because she did not stop it or say anything. So I took her to the neighbor's townhome and made her apologize for the egging. I did not remember doing this. She told me I did and she remembered the lesson she learned because of it, to respect the rights and property of others. When children would throw trash or damage flowers or trees she would reprimand them and chase them away when she was still a child.

I wasn't perfect as a parent. After Jasmine's father left and I was going to college, working multiple jobs, struggling to pay all the bills while taking care of a 20 month old, I admit I was stressed. At a well-baby check Jasmine's pediatrician recommended I have counseling. I did go to counseling and it helped. When Jasmine cried, as she did every evening, I hugged her and cried with her.

I was as emotional as Jasmine and had to really learn how to control my reaction to the times she got in trouble at school. When Jasmine was older she became reluctant to tell me and then I would get more upset when I found out she did not tell me something I found out from the school later. So I told her no matter what it was to let me know because it was more difficult to deal with if she did not tell me than if she did, and I worked on staying calm, unemotional and remaining supportive when these type of things happened.

Every year since Jasmine was born my sister and I saw three plays at the Colorado Shakespeare Festival. Jasmine always went with us. She actually attended when she was three months old. When she was seven I bought her a book for each of the plays we would be seeing written in a comic book style but in Elizabethan language. The books were rated for nine year olds. She read the books. Then she asked me if she could read the plays in the regular Shakespeare book. I gave her my college text "Shakespeare's Complete Works" to read. She then read the plays again.

I had heard that it is good to have your child read to you to see how well she reads and understands what she is reading. I picked out a passage in "Shakespeare's Complete Works" and asked Jasmine to read it. She read it unhesitatingly with the proper inflection. I then asked her what the passage meant and she summarized it exactly as was intended.

When she was in the theater before the play one time, Jasmine overheard a couple asking each other if they had seen the play or if they knew what it was about. Neither of them had seen nor read the play. Jasmine proceeded to explain the play to the couple.

By October shortly after school started in the third grade, the Principal told me Jasmine was emotionally disturbed and had to be seen by a mental health professional. I told her I did not know where to take her since the HMO would not see her. I was told to take her to Catholic Charities for counseling. The counselor there said that was not something he was trained to do and suggested I take her to see the psychologist at the public school. The psychologist was very nice and said he would evaluate her and it would take an hour unless there was something that needed more time. It took an hour and a half. When he was finished he asked me what problems she was having in school. I told him she was distracting the others in class and not paying attention. He said she is bored in school. She had knowledge of math that she had not learned yet. When the psychologist asked her how she knew how to divide she said it was obvious. The reason the session took so long was Jasmine was able to continue on and on. She tested in the very superior range with an overall IQ of 138, a mean of 100, and a standard deviation of 15; which meant she was two and a half standard deviations above the mean in the 99th percentile. Her verbal score was 143. The psychologist said she could read anything at the age of eight. He also said the teachers and principal would be wise to attempt to understand Jasmine and where she is coming from.

I did three things.

I told Jasmine she thought very differently than most other people; that there would be few who would understand her. Also that her biggest challenge would be getting along with people who were not as intelligent as she is but had authority over her like bosses and teachers. I told her she was not better than others but that she would be able to do things others couldn't do and that everyone has aptitude in certain areas and that is the way it should be; that people not as intelligent as she would be able to complete tasks that would be very mind-numbing to her.

I gave the extensive written report to the private school Principal. I subsequently took her out of private school and put her in the public school where she saw the psychologist because the Principal said "if she is so smart then she should be able to..." They actually wanted to hold her back a year because they said she wasn't emotionally able to handle third grade. She had problems at the private school because it was a traditional school with three months off in the summer. A lot of time at the beginning of the new school year was spent reviewing from the previous year. Jasmine did not forget from the previous year and had difficulty understanding why she had to relearn the same things. Another unfortunate result of the Principal's and teachers' poor opinion of

Jasmine and the way they treated her, the students in the school started mistreating her, bullying her, as well.

I went to the HMO mental health department and insisted they assign her to the best therapist available since they obviously misdiagnosed her three years previously; and they did.

The damage had been done. The Principal and teachers told Jasmine she was a bad person because of her behavior (an evil child). When I talked to Jasmine I found she actually believed she was a bad person. I told her the teachers and Principal were not used to the type of person she was and they saw this as bad but that she was not bad but different in a way they did not understand. The other children saw her being treated as a bad person by the school staff and began bullying her as well. Jasmine was angry and defensive instead of happy and fun loving as she had been. I resolved from that time forward to go with my intuition instead of listening to others especially when it involved my daughter.

It was around this time that I attended a class on "Parenting The Difficult Child." The major lesson I learned from that class was "pick your battles."

We were in a single parents' group at the church when Jasmine was in private school. It was a group of single mothers and fathers with their children. We had Thanksgiving dinners together and took trips to the mountains. One of the mothers told me my daughter had hurt her son. She had two sons, one Jasmine's age and one four years older. The older boy was picking on Jasmine and she hit him. I was surprised that she was able to stand up to someone so much older; however, I apologized to his mother for her but did mention Jasmine did not start things but she was not afraid to finish them.

Elementary School

———— ❦ ————

Jasmine cried that she had to leave the private school mostly because she didn't like change. I didn't know if public school would be better for her either, but I hoped at least she would be able to get away from the evil child label.

Jasmine started in public school halfway through the third grade and continued to see the school psychologist in her new school. The two teachers she had in third and fourth grade understood her. One of the teachers had been a gifted, intelligent, child herself. They made it very clear to Jasmine what the rules were in the school. The school was a year-around school, which means she was in school for a certain number of weeks then off for three weeks all year long. There was no need for extensive review when the students returned and the school had an after school care and care during the three weeks off that could be purchased. She was at a disadvantage though. She was a new student, starting in the middle of the year and because of the bullying by the teachers and then the students in the private school she was defensive.

The teachers and staff in the public elementary school did a good job ensuring the students did not bully each other. However, one winter Jasmine had two coats disappear at school. Since it was April I told her I would buy her a new coat in the fall. I was called by the school and told she needed a coat. I said she had two coats both of which had gone missing at school and I would buy her a new coat for the fall. Amazingly, after that call both coats turned up in the lost and found.

Jasmine was suspended a day for throwing a pair of scissors at a girl who was bullying her. The staff said both girls were counseled for their behavior but since throwing sharp objects at another student could be dangerous, Jasmine was suspended for one day. On other occasions when Jasmine was bullied and the other student made accusations, the teachers would question the student as to what did you do to her, Jasmine never starts things, but she will finish them.

Jasmine experienced an interest in sexuality around this time. I had a book "Human Sexuality" that I gave her to read. It discussed everything that was available to know about human sexuality. This knowledge served her well. However, I did have to tell her not to share the information with her classmates.

The teachers were not fond of my efforts to encourage independence. I was called once because Jasmine wasn't wearing socks and that they understood because I was a single parent and probably did not have time to wash socks. I told them that Jasmine was responsible for ensuring that her socks got into the wash and when she didn't and didn't have clean socks she would learn to be responsible for getting her socks in the laundry.

I was also called because she didn't have lunch and could I bring her lunch to her. I told the teacher that I was not able to leave my job; that Jasmine was responsible for taking her lunch and that not having lunch for one day would inspire her to bring it the next day. She won't starve. She whined so much they came up with some crackers for her and made sure crackers were on hand for children that forgot their lunch. Shortly thereafter they started to offer a hot lunch and the problem was solved.

Jasmine had an opportunity to be in the school play when she was in fourth grade. She was the only fourth grader in the play, the other actors were in fifth and sixth grade. The play was one that she dearly loved: "A Christmas Carol" by Charles Dickens. She was the Ghost of Christmas Present. I made her a robe just like the one worn by the Ghost of Christmas Present in the 1984 movie. We had it on video and she watched it constantly.

Of course she had already memorized her lines since she recited them along with the video. She was able to remain in character though when the microphone hiccupped.

She had a different teacher in fifth and sixth grade, a male teacher. She had an option to go to a different school for sixth grade. Since she was still nervous about new things she stayed at the elementary school for sixth grade. Her new teacher wasn't as understanding of her as the two women were who taught her in third and fourth grade.

She did however have an opportunity to be a part of a study which involved all the students getting laptops in fifth grade. The laptop was a Tandy with two floppy drives so it wasn't a laptop like the ones available today. She wasn't unfamiliar with computers even at that age. She had access to a computer in the day care when she was four and I had an Adam computer at the same time to use for my graduate studies in finance and information systems. She had a Smurf game on my computer. She also learned how to use an Apple IIe in private school. She was so enamored of the laptop that she wanted one of her own to use outside of school.

Unfortunately Jasmine was still an angry, defensive child, especially in fifth and sixth grade. She began therapy in third grade and was in several therapy groups to help her interact better with her peers. It was difficult for me to watch her have difficulty with other children at this age when she was so happy and confident at the age of four. Having been bullied she was defensive and this caused her to be bullied even more.

Jasmine was still insecure and would not sleep in her own bed until a classmate who lived near us needed to find a new home for an older cat. We took in the cat and named her Otis. Of course Otis needed a companion, so we found a four month old tiny calico cat at the Dumb Friends League to keep her company. Jasmine was very excited about the little cat and named her Maranatha after a song she heard at church. From that time forward she would sleep in her own bed with little Maranatha, Mara for short, at her side.

Jasmine was in a soccer league fourth through sixth grade. She was a good performer in soccer. On the soccer field she often played even though her heel bones were painful. She was growing very fast and was bigger and stronger than all of the girls on her team. She could kick the soccer ball $\frac{3}{4}$ of the length of the field and when she kicked the ball the other girls dove out of the way of the ball.

Jasmine, my mom, my sister and I went to Boston when Jasmine was 12 for a Titanic Historical Society convention at her request. We stayed at a historic hotel where Jasmine was able to experience an English Tea Room. We visited the local sites, including Harvard. Jasmine got the autographs of the remaining Titanic survivors at the convention on her convention badge. She has it to this day.

This was one of the many road trips I, my sister Sophie, my Mom and Jasmine we went on during summer vacations. As Jasmine got older, her cousin Roxanne came with us so Jasmine would have someone her age to explore with. We traveled all over Colorado, Arizona, Utah and South Dakota.

Of course we made many trips to Illinois near Chicago to visit Jasmine's grandparents, aunts, uncles and cousins. She was especially interested in the Art Institute of Chicago and the various museums.

We toured California including Disneyland. Some of the other trips we took were to Portland, Oregon; Louisville, Kentucky; Greensboro, North Carolina; and Buffalo, New York. On the trip to New York, Jasmine, her aunt and grandmother took a train to New York City, and she saw for the first time Manhattan and the Statue of Liberty. We visited Toronto, Canada, on this trip as well. The border guard in Canada wanted to know where we were from. The only one he questioned was Jasmine, he wanted to know where she was born, since she did not look like the rest of us because of her Mexican coloring.

We also crossed the border into Mexico in Yuma, Arizona. We had to have a birth certificate for Jasmine. In those days passports were not required for Canada or Mexico.

Jasmine looked just like the majority of the people in Yuma, Arizona, and across the border in San Luis, Mexico. This was also true on Indian reservations in Utah and New Mexico. A tourist asked if he could take Jasmine's picture next to a Hogan. We had difficulty finding her in the store on the reservation, she looked exactly like all of the other Indians.

We visited Washington DC. Jasmine was especially excited about the Museums of the Smithsonian. She did not want to stay with the slow old folks and met us at a designated location.

Middle School

———— ❦ ————

Middle school was very difficult for Jasmine. She attended Middle school for only seventh and eighth grade. Initially she told me she was going to be a mood ring and whatever mood the other kids in the school came at her with she would duplicate it. I told her is that really what you want. Do you believe doing what the others are doing is being true to the way that you really feel.

Jasmine was spit upon, pushed off the bus, had rocks thrown at her, and bullied and called names constantly. I made an appointment with her counselor. He told me that the other students did not like her because she wasn't like them. I told him from her perspective, why would she want to be like people who were mean and nasty to others. He said that's how kids are, he was the same way in school. Jasmine said she did not understand why she had to be a sacrificial lamb to their rite of passage.

The school counselor encouraged me to get counseling for Jasmine. Jasmine was in counseling and had been for many years so she could understand why others found it necessary to make her life a living hell.

Jasmine had her own style. She designed her own clothes and I sewed them for her. She wore skirts because they looked better on her. She did like her Minnitonka moccasins. She did not feel inclined to dress the way the other students did.

If Jasmine talked to the other students in her normal way of speaking they would say she was talking down to them. If she attempted to talk to them more in line with how they spoke they would say she was talking down to them. However, she did get along with the special needs students.

Even though Jasmine tested at grade 17 reading level in eight grade, which would put her at a postgraduate college reading level, Jasmine was put in a remedial reading class. Then the teacher would complain that she would bring in other books to read. She was in that class for one semester. I convinced them she would do better in advanced English. She was put in advanced English the next semester and did well. She was also not allowed to take a foreign language although the requirement to take a foreign language was two reading levels above grade level.

That Jasmine was always asking the teachers "when are you going to teach me something I do not already know" did not go over well with them. One of her teachers did recognize something in her though and asked her to grade papers for her. This gave Jasmine confidence.

Jasmine was interested in calligraphy in middle school which morphed into her doing illuminating, like the art the Monks did in the bibles long ago. While Jasmine was not an actor in "A Christmas Carol" in seventh grade, she did create the artwork for the program. Jasmine made a little money with her illuminating abilities by creating illuminated names for her classmates. She even used gold leaf in her illuminations for special purposes.

I enrolled her in a team building ropes course that was suggested by the school so she could learn to interact better with the other students. The only thing she remembers about the experience is that they dropped one of the other students. Fortunately they were wearing harnesses.

Jasmine also volunteered during the summers at the Molly Brown House in Denver, Colorado, as a tour page who assisted the tour guide with keeping the guests in the authorized portions of the house. The clothes she liked to wear fit in with the period with little modification. As I said previously Jasmine impressed the staff so much with her knowledge of the sinking of the Titanic that the guides deferred to her when Molly Brown's experience on the Titanic came up.

She also attended the YMCA camp during the summers at Camp Chief Ouray so she could learn how to interact with other campers.

She actually had fairly good grades in elementary and middle school considering her problems which resulted from being bullied. She always did well in following rules, her reading was consistently above grade level, and she was always not working up to her ability. Of course how much she worked at a subject depended on her interest in it. She received an award for a Geography Bee in elementary school.

At home Jasmine became a latchkey kid. She came home from school, let herself in the house and waited for me or my sister to come home to make dinner. For the most part she didn't have any problems other than the egging situation mentioned previously and an incident that happened which inspired me to tell her not to show her knife collection to the neighborhood kids. They were not as able as she was to handle knives. She could usually be found in her room curled up with Mara, reading.

Jasmine quickly decided that waiting until someone came home to eat wasn't working for her so she called my office. I wasn't at my desk; however, she told Ralph, a single fellow I worked with, that she wanted to make stew and needed to know how. Ralph explained how to make stew to her over the phone and we came home to a hot bowl of stew that evening. She did the cooking all the time after that with a little more instruction on how to make her other favorites.

Another incident happened when she was a latchkey kid. The toilet upstairs ran over. Jasmine turned off the water to the toilet; however, water still got on the floor and went into the air vent. This caused the downstairs smoke detector to short out and go off. Jasmine did not know if there was an actual fire or not but she evacuated all the animals to the back porch and then called me. I told her it was probably a short and told her how to turn off the breaker to the smoke detector. Everything turned out okay except the large male rabbit and the dwarf female rabbit got together which caused the tiny female rabbit to have a very large stillborn baby rabbit. My sister had the male rabbit neutered after that.

High School

———— ◦❀◦ ————

Jasmine attended the high school she would have normally attended for the geographic area where we lived. The school had an International Baccalaureate (IB) program which I thought would allow Jasmine to be more challenged and hopefully more successful in school.

Unfortunately that was not the case.

Jasmine continued to be bullied unmercifully. She came home every day upset and depressed about how she was treated. There was one boy, a Jewish boy, who would tell the others to leave Jasmine alone that she had had enough. Jasmine said only the Jewish students stood up for her and she took instructions in the Jewish religion for a while because of that.

It was 1993, the year the Pope came to Colorado for World Youth Day in August. Jasmine took part in the World Youth Day festivities as part of a group from the church where she had attended elementary school in the beginning. She was having difficulty as part of the group and walked off by herself in downtown Denver. She did rejoin the group and came back safely.

Later in the year I heard about a Catholic youth trip to Munich that was leaving from a nearby boys Catholic high school. I signed Jasmine up for the trip and she went on the trip. The majority of attendees were boys from the school, a few other girls and some parents and young adults as chaperones. Jasmine did well on this trip. She was with a smaller group of boys and young adults who had Scottish and Irish heritage in common. Two of the boys played the bagpipe. In Germany the drinking age is 14 so Jasmine was able to sample Guinness beer and Bailey's Irish Crème at the Irish pub in Munich on their free time from the religious event. The group also visited the Neuschwanstein Castle in Schwangau, Germany, and the Dachau Concentration Camp.

This experience saved Jasmine. She now had something to focus on and look forward to when she returned home. She immediately sought out and joined the Scottish Saint Andrews Society, visited a bagpipe band, found a store selling Scottish and bagpipe items, and bought a bagpipe chanter and beginner's book. She was able to play the first few tunes by the time we arrived at home.

Jasmine began bagpipe lessons with two men: one for bagpipe band and competition tunes and one for pobaireachd (pronounced pe brook), a more classical and soulful sounding version of bagpipe. She began competing at the first level, grade four, the following summer and won and/or placed in a few competitions. She competed every summer during high school and moved up in the competitions. She also played with a number of bands, joined an Irish band and did band competitions with that band. She won or placed in competitions out of state as well including at a pobaireachd competition in Reno, Nevada.

Since Jasmine could perform well on the bagpipe, it gave her a way to increase her confidence and self-esteem. She had no contact with her father since he left before she was two years old, so the men she studied bagpipe with and assisted her with her competitions were a positive male influence in her life.

I said the bagpipe saved Jasmine because her high school experience was primarily a nightmare.

While she did fairly well in math before, she got straight Fs in math in high school. Since no one at the high school was forthcoming with any help, I enrolled Jasmine in the Sylvan Learning Center so she could get extra help in math. The assessment done at Sylvan identified problems with math concepts that Jasmine should have learned in fifth grade. She quickly progressed with math at Sylvan.

Jasmine started taking German in freshman year in high school. However, the language requirement for the IB program was five years of German, so after two years of German Jasmine was told she needed to make up the year of German she missed because she was not allowed to take a foreign language in middle school. The choices were a summer study program abroad or enroll in a college course. The summer study abroad program cost more than I was prepared to spend so I enrolled Jasmine in my alma mater to take the third course in German in the summer after her sophomore year.

In the German college class, Jasmine was amazed that no one refused to be in a group with her, no one criticized her clothing, and no one made fun of her or called her names in the class. The instructor said she did not learn everything in the first two years in high school that was required to take the third class in college; however, he told her she would have no problem learning the additional material. She got an A in her college course in German.

She had grade point averages between 1.3 and 2.0 all throughout high school.

Jasmine was suspended a few times for not attending class, opting instead to practice her chanter in the hallway. She received an award for her writing at the same time that the school authorities were flunking her in English.

She was not allowed in the computer room because the school administration said she was stalking another student.

She was not allowed on the campus after hours primarily because when a teacher who was criticizing her for practicing her chanter and not focusing more on her studies told her if she did not like it she could leave, she left and did not come back to class. She told the other students they only have authority over us if we allow them to. So the school administration considered her an anarchist although she had always respected authority, credible authority that is. The authorities probably were also concerned that other students were picking up on her fashion sense and starting to wear capes. She learned to ignore the bullies and assisted the other students she felt she could help.

My thought that Jasmine's independence would serve her was borne out in high school. I let Jasmine attend functions the other students weren't allowed by their parents to attend. When they wanted to know why, I said that it was a school sanctioned event and I could trust Jasmine to behave appropriately. When the other students wanted Jasmine to sneak out and go to a Rave she told them "she could forego it." When she would have a problem the other students would tell her to call her Mom. Jasmine told them "she will just tell me it's a personal problem and you can handle it." And she would handle it. Yes she did have friends. One girl lived near us the first two years of high school. Then she went to another school. One friend moved to the area from Arizona in Jasmine's junior year. She and Jasmine are still friends.

Around this time Jasmine experienced an incident with authority at a retreat for confirmandi, young people who are about to be confirmed in the Catholic Church. Jasmine was of the opinion retreats were characterized by silence and self-reflection. The people holding the retreat had a different opinion and wanted the confirmandi to share their thoughts. Jasmine shared her thoughts as instructed – in German. She attended the confirmation ceremony and just as for her communion ceremony her behavior was appropriate to the occasion.

As I said previously Jasmine could read at a very early age and she would bring books to read in church, just the latest novel she was reading. Other people at church would openly make remarks or give dirty looks. When she complained about this I told her that is one of the consequences of doing something different in church. Jasmine would tell me "the readings were about this, the gospel was about this, and the sermon was about this. Do the people criticizing me know? If they were paying attention to the mass as they should they would not notice me reading."

I was criticized for allowing Jasmine to read in church. I would tell the people, trust me, it is better that she read in church otherwise she would be more distracting. This was more difficult for me than it would seem. I was verbally abused or beaten if I did anything that would be noticed in public when I was young. I was afraid to rock back and forth (I found out not that long ago this is called stimming and is normal behavior for people on the autistic spectrum) or otherwise self-sooth and even now it takes an immense amount of energy for me to avoid these behaviors. I still have post-traumatic stress disorder (PTSD) like reactions to any type of attention from others because of what I knew I would be subjected to at home for it when I was younger. It doesn't go away. I would not treat my daughter in this way and when I saw her reaction to her father treating her this way when I was not around I asked him to leave. Jasmine was crying without making any sounds just as I did as a child.

Jasmine deliberately flunked two courses in high school. One was health because the teacher was handing out condoms and she disagreed with that. The other class was a computer class that she liked. One day she left the class to go to the restroom and was surprised when she was called to the principal's office. She was sent there because she violated a rule – to ask the teacher for permission before she went to the restroom. This was a rule; however, the rule was not consistently followed in every class, so to Jasmine it was not a rule at all. I was called to a conference with the teacher who told me that Jasmine was flunking her class and she didn't know why. She assumed I didn't know either because, of course, I was a single parent. I told her I knew exactly why Jasmine was flunking her class. Jasmine expected the teacher to tell her that there was a rule that she was now enforcing about asking permission before getting up to go to the restroom. Since the teacher said nothing to her, and instead sent her directly to the principal, Jasmine did not consider her a credible authority and was deliberately flunking her class. I told the teacher that was her choice to make and I let her make her own choices.

In the summers Jasmine had taken two geometry courses in another school district, the German course in college and a Russian course in a community college. She performed better in these situations than she did in her high school so she was not hurting for credits. She also had credits for the Sylvan instruction. In one of the geometry courses Jasmine, as always, had her bagpipe chanter with her to play on breaks. She came back from the restroom to find the chanter on the teacher's desk in two pieces. One of the other students had taken it from her backpack and separated the two pieces. The teacher insisted the student who had done this come forward thinking the chanter was broken. When the students complained that Jasmine shouldn't have brought it to school if she did not want it touched, the teacher said that Jasmine had a right to her property and her interests and they did not have a right to disturb her possessions. Jasmine got Bs in those two geometry courses. The teacher said she was still not working up to her potential. What a difference this was from the school she normally attended.

In her senior year she dropped out of the IB program. She had a 1.3 GPA. She had a very difficult time with the constant bullying which now included stealing her things. The school administration told her that they could do nothing about the other students' behavior toward her and that she had to somehow get used to it, get over it, take counseling and start working harder at her studies or she would never get into college. I told her Einstein did poorly in high school and he, nevertheless, was successful in life and she could be too. I told her she could continue to go to high school or since she was having such difficulty she could drop out and get a GED. She stayed in high school. She loved to learn.

She did learn something in the IB program, however. The IB program attracted intelligent and gifted students from the entire district so there were a few who were on her intellectual level. She found out that even though the other students were intelligent, they weren't good at everything. Everyone needed to study and learn some things. She had always assumed that if she didn't already know things, it would impossible or difficult to learn them. Jasmine took it upon herself to tutor the students who weren't native English speakers in English in the IB program.

I was not told that Jasmine would be graduating with the senior class until about a week before school ended. She was able to attend commencement with her class and I was there to see her graduate as she was to see me graduate with my bachelor and master degrees.

I dropped out of college when Jasmine was born after completing my Spanish class requirements over the phone for the remaining four weeks of the semester. I was inspired to return to school after Jasmine's father lost his job and told me that I could sell myself for extra money. I knew I would be able to do better than that. I told him to leave after the semester was over. I had gotten a raise and promotion at work and was barely able to cover all the bills. I had one year to go in college and the next semester I had a required meeting with the school counselor. I told her I might have to drop out because I couldn't afford the tuition any more. She told me scholarships were now available for part time; she called the financial aid office and told them to wait for me. The financial aid clerk told me the application deadline was the next day, gave me the application to complete, and told me a 500 word essay was also required. I wrote the essay on the bus on the way home, typed it with my typing jobs the next morning and turned it in after I got off work. I got the scholarship and was able to continue my education through graduate school on merit scholarships. I had to do what I could to make a better life for my baby. She was six when I finished graduate school.

Post High School

---- ❧ ----

In the summer after graduation, Jasmine went to Poland on a Habitat for Humanity build with her grandmother and her aunt. She used the money I had put away for college for her to join them on the trip. She did a good job there. My mother spoke Polish; Jasmine did not. However, during their free time, Jasmine went off by herself on a bus to go shopping. Some of the Polish shopkeepers knew German so Jasmine was able to communicate with them having had five years of German. One of the side trips Jasmine, her grandma and aunt took while in Poland was to the concentration camp Auschwitz in Oswiecim, Poland. I would think not many people have visited even one concentration camp but by the age of 19 Jasmine had visited two, as well as the Holocaust Memorial Museum in Washington, D.C.

Interestingly Jasmine had no problem being accepted into colleges with her 1.3 GPA. She had a 27 score on the ACT and was accepted in a history degree program. I paid for her first semester; however, I told her that college would mean more to her if she found a way to pay for it on her own.

She got a job at a Chick-Fil-A. Jasmine learned a lot on that job: how to clean, how to handle the drive-through, and how to communicate with others. She was the only crew member who could run the drive-through on her own without help. She did have to convince the people in the back actually making the food that her method would only work with their cooperation in getting the food to her on time.

Since she was now working and I was planning on a trip in a few months, it was time for Jasmine to learn to drive. She was eager to learn when she was 15 until we were in an accident. A car slammed into us, Jasmine's head slammed into my head and my head broke out the side window. After that she was very reluctant to learn to drive. I taught Jasmine to drive like I taught myself to drive. Instead of letting her back out in our townhome parking lot, I drove to a large church parking lot where Jasmine said the police practiced with their motorcycles. She had seen them there when she was taking the bus. In the parking lot she learned how to start the car, start off slowly, back up, pull into a parking space, and handle the car's steering. I always drove manuals and the car Jasmine learned on was a manual.

She passed her driver's test and got her license so she could drive herself to work when I was on the trip. When I returned, she told me she had also driven to Boulder, 30 miles away from home, to go to the Shakespeare Festival on her own. However, she was still a little timid so I enrolled her in a two day Master Drive course. She gained much more confidence in driving from the course which was both a blessing and a curse. It was a blessing because she avoided several accidents with other vehicles and was also able to handle some nasty skids on ice. It was a curse because she was so confident that she began speeding and began to rack up the tickets and points. Still she took responsibility. She told me she went to the court for a speeding ticket and was asked how she pled. She said guilty. The judge was flabbergasted. Jasmine told him "my Mama always told me I am responsible for my actions, I was speeding, what's my fine." She had the same attitude toward library fines, although sometimes she would wait for the amnesty period to bring in her many overdue books.

Jasmine's aunt Sophie moved to her own home because her new job required her to live in Denver. Sophie also was dating a man she met when singing in a chorale. She married Paul in 1999 at the age of 52. The first marriage for both of them. Jasmine and I were on our own.

Along with the history, Jasmine started taking courses in Russian. She quickly outgrew the college she was attending and went to another college with an actual minor in Russian.

During the summer she went on several school sponsored, professor-led trips to Russia. She liked the idea of giving tours and this was when she first had the idea of becoming a professor. This was also when she decided never to drink again. On one of the Russian tours she was on a long river boat ride, the liquor was flowing freely, she over-imbibed and became very sick. She survived this experience and vowed never to drink alcohol again.

Jasmine's professors told her if she really wanted to focus on Russian she would have to find a college with a major in Russian. She said none of the local colleges had a good Russian program so, without visiting the campus ahead of time, she enrolled in Indiana University, in Bloomington, Indiana.

Jasmine met a young man in a Russian class. She was helping a study group of foreign students understand Russian. She married him; however, they quickly grew apart and eventually divorced. The cultural differences were undoubtedly a factor. Jasmine was also very independent and nothing would stop her from doing what she wanted to do.

Driving was still fairly new to her so I drove nearly the entire distance to Bloomington in one day. We stopped in a nearby town late at night and rented a motel room. When Jasmine was little she would sleep in the car and when she got older she became sleepy on long car rides. This is not good for someone who has to drive. She said she drove fast because it kept her on edge so she would not get sleepy. Eventually she lost her license because of too many points. Fortunately she did not need her license because she was leaving for Indiana.

I drove her to the campus the next morning and helped her move her things into the dorm. She had arranged for a dorm room by herself, with no roommate. I was ready to leave to go to my Mom's house in Illinois then to get the road trip over and relax, but she wanted me to stay with her and tour the campus. I was happy to visit the campus with her; however, she says I was just going to drop her off and run.

Jasmine did well in college in Bloomington as she did in the two other colleges. She was taking courses that interested her. She took a course in linguistics that helped her with the many languages she would be taking. She worked in the campus cafeteria as well.

By the end of the semester Jasmine was ready to move on. She said the college focused mainly on training CIA agents and she was ready for more in depth Russian courses. So Jasmine contacted the State School in Saint Petersburg, Russia, got a passport and Visa and went to Saint Petersburg, Russia, the following semester. I had to help her a little with the money but she budgeted it wisely while she was there. She was fairly confident speaking Russian; however, she hired an interpreter when she opened a bank account. It didn't hurt that everything was cheaper and the exchange rate was good.

At first Jasmine stayed in the dorm at the university, but eventually got an apartment of her own because the dorm was very noisy and distracting. Of course the apartment wasn't up to her standards and she had a little remodeling done. Jasmine was a good tenant and got along well with her landlady.

One of the benefits of being a student in the Russian State School and not a student in a foreign program was Jasmine was able to take advantage of the many museums, like the Hermitage, and concerts and ballet at the Russian student rate. She attended them often.

I only remember hearing from Jasmine in the roughly ten months she was in Saint Petersburg twice. Once she wanted some recipes because she was having her friends over for dinner. She had friends from several countries.

Jasmine fit in well wherever she went. She did not look American and could pass for Italian or even Russian. Her accent gave her away though. The other time she was going to be coming home soon and wanted to know what I wanted her to bring me. I asked for a Matryoshka or Russian nesting doll. If I had known that she was going to walk all over town in freezing weather looking for just the right doll and almost freeze to death I would have told her I could forego it for her safety, but she didn't tell me until she got back home.

While Jasmine was in Saint Petersburg she visited Stockholm, Sweden, which is just a ferry ride across the Baltic Sea. I believe she was in Sweden staying in a hostel when 9-11 occurred. She said the others came and got her because they knew she was American and told her America was under attack. She watched it unfold on the television there.

When Jasmine arrived home she announced that she wanted to travel to Sweden to study Swedish and possibly attend college there. She said college is free for everyone in Sweden. She studied Swedish on her own for three months then went to Stockholm, Sweden, and enrolled in the Swedish language program for non-Swedes. All of the students in the program were not new to the country, some had been in Sweden for years. Jasmine took a placement test and was placed in level five of seven. At times the Swedish instructor would ask Jasmine how she would explain some aspect of the language to the students. Her course in linguistics was very helpful. Swedish is a Germanic language, and having studied German for five years, Jasmine found Swedish fairly easy to learn.

Jasmine applied to all the colleges in Sweden and was accepted in all of them. This was unusual because the Swedish colleges rely on high school scores rather than later college scores. Remember Jasmine had a 1.3 GPA in her senior year in high school.

Nevertheless, when Jasmine returned from Sweden she had already decided that getting into a graduate program in an America college with a Swedish degree would not work. She learned that the University of Colorado, Boulder, had instituted a good Russian program in both language and literature and she enrolled in college there.

She was still working and going to school. Jasmine got a job at Falafel King, where she learned to do food prep and also acquired a taste for hummus and falafels. She even bought herself a professional chef prep knife to use at work. She had difficulty with one of her bosses. This upset her because it was reminiscent of her high school years and because of this her grades slipped for one semester. The supervisor relegated Jasmine to the back of the restaurant to do only prep work saying she didn't have the appropriate people skills. He finally fired her. Jasmine went to counseling after this happened of her own accord. She determined that the boss that fired her was wrong about her people skills.

She got a job as a barista at a Starbucks in an Albertsons close to home. She became an expert at the various drinks. Jasmine also learned how to clean the machines properly. Jasmine always milked all the learning possible out of a job and did everything exceptionally well. She was frequently the only person opening and/or closing the Starbucks and she knew everything about the operation. She quit when she was passed over for a supervisor position.

Jasmine realized that jobs were plentiful in locations that were just opening so she applied at a Wild Oats market, subsequently bought out by Whole Foods, that was just opening. When she interviewed for the position she was asked her background. She told the manager that she was descended from Polish immigrants in Chicago. The manager said the work ethic of Polish people from Chicago was legendary and she was given the position based on this alone. Her job was as an assistant in the meat department. She learned, as usual, everything there was to know about meat, fish, cuts of meat, preparation of meat, etc.

Jasmine did have issues with the jobs she had in phone sales. She was conscientious about the work but she and her bosses had philosophical and ethical differences with regard to convincing callers to buy when they obviously were not interested.

Jasmine was progressing well in college although her GPA took a little hit because of the trauma with the Falafel King Manager. Her professor in the Russian literature program told her if she was serious about attending graduate school she should finish her undergraduate by the following year. She took four courses in the summer and a full load in the spring. She applied to the six universities her professor recommended. She also had to take the GRE exam.

Jasmine also had to submit a writing sample. She decided she wanted to visit her grandparents on her father's side in Yuma, Arizona. She finished the writing sample on the trip to Yuma, I was driving of course, and she emailed it to the colleges from a hotel on the way, this was before wifi was common. Jasmine's relatives on her father's side did not understand her attending graduate school. Only a very few of Jasmine's relatives attended and/or completed high school and some did not complete elementary school.

Jasmine was asked to come to all six campuses she applied to for a visit. Since Jasmine is half Mexican her campus visits were paid for by the schools. This is the only consideration she received for her ethnicity. After the campus visits she was offered full fellowships for a Russian Literature Ph.D. program in five of the six universities. The comments made by the schools were that her writing sample was ingenious. The work in Russian she wrote about was supposedly a work of fiction and she made a good case for it being nonfiction.

I attended her commencement from college. It was a department commencement and Jasmine's professor said Jasmine was the only person in the school who applied for and received five out of six full fellowships. The schools Jasmine applied to were University of California at Berkeley, Northwestern in Chicago, Columbia University in Manhattan, Harvard, University of Wisconsin, and University of Ohio. Jasmine said she did not interview well at Harvard and that was the college that did not offer her a fellowship. Because of her dip that one semester Jasmine had a 3.3 GPA. Harvard went by GPA primarily.

Jasmine chose Columbia. She felt it was a better fit for her learning style and it was. The one drawback was its location in Manhattan. Jasmine is Colorado born and raised and she enjoys the open spaces, the expansive malls, and the scenery. She was definitely not fond of the concrete jungle.

In the summer before Jasmine attended Columbia she and her best friend toured Europe. She funded this by having her father declared dead so she could get his $25,000 life insurance death benefit. She had been talking with a friend and told her she had not seen her father since she was six years old when she had asked her Nana if she could see him when we were visiting her grandparents. Her Nana found him in Mexico and brought him to her friend's house so Jasmine could visit for a short while. Jasmine found the new litter of puppies at the home more interesting. The friend told her she could have him declared dead so she could get his life insurance. I had been paying for this group policy all along and said I would be glad not to have to pay it anymore. Jasmine would be the beneficiary since her father and I are divorced. Jasmine contacted her grandparents who verified he had not been seen in years. In Colorado it is only necessary to show he had not been heard from in five years.

That summer was unfortunately when Mara died. She had gotten cancer and was riddled with tumors. Jasmine even took her to the animal hospital at the University in Fort Collins, but nothing could be done. One Sunday morning Mara woke up and could not move her hind legs. She was terrified and began dragging herself to Jasmine's room. Jasmine was not home, she had stayed at her friend's house overnight. I called Jasmine and told her Mara needed her, then I went to church. When I got home Jasmine was berating me for being gone and that we needed to take Mara to the emergency vet so she would not have to suffer any longer. We had our hands on Mara when she was given the shot to put her to sleep.

Jasmine said we need to get a cat for me since she would be going to Europe and then to Columbia. Jasmine, always the researcher, said there were no tabby cats to be found in Denver so we drove to the Fort Collins Humane Society and found Serenity, a two year old grey tabby.

Another example of Jasmine's stellar research abilities is the occasion when my mother wanted a book on Blessed Mary Angela Truszkowska, the foundress of the Polish Felician Sisters religious order, for her sister who was a Felician Sister. No one could find a book on this woman on line even my brother-in-law the civil engineer. So I asked Jasmine to see if she could find a book. After about five minutes Jasmine asked me "what language would you like it in; there were books written about her in Vietnamese, French, Polish and English." I said English will be fine.

When Jasmine was touring France she visited a pet shop and found a little brown male tabby cat she fell in love with. She bought the cat and carried him all through Europe sometimes walking him on a leash. She named him Valera, a Russian name. Valera loved to travel and loved the attention he got from everyone. After Jasmine and

Valera came home, Jasmine went to New York to find an apartment. She couldn't stay in the dorms on campus with a pet and she learned from her Russian experience that dorms were not conducive to study.

Valera stayed with me until Jasmine found an apartment, then I and Jasmine's friend Dolores drove a moving van to New York with furniture Jasmine had bought ahead of time. Valera was on the lap of whoever wasn't driving. We had a pan with cat litter under the seat that we brought out when we stopped so Valera could do his business. He was a good traveler.

We stayed at my Mom's halfway, which was right off the highway, then stopped at a motel at night so we could get to Jasmine's Manhattan apartment very early in the morning. Fortunately there were two open parking spaces in front of her building when we arrived where we could park the moving van. We unloaded the van and got everything into her apartment. The building fortunately had an elevator, because she was on the fifth floor. I had the pleasure of driving the moving van nearly the entire length of Broadway to return it to the rental company.

In her apartment once Jasmine heard a woman being raped in the hallway outside of her apartment and called the police. She was amazed when detectives from the Special Victims Unit came to interview her. She loved to watch Special Victims Unit on television and was excited that she actually got to meet the real thing. The rape victim was okay because one of Jasmine's neighbors came out of his apartment naked and surprised the perpetrator.

Just as in Saint Petersburg, Jasmine's Columbia student ID gave her free access to museums and art galleries. She loved to tour the museums and especially the art galleries.

Jasmine's program at Columbia involved her taking courses in Russian literature, teaching beginning Russian courses, completing a Master's Thesis for her first Master's in Russian Literature, taking comprehensive tests for her second Master's in Russian Literature, and completing a Dissertation for her Ph.D. in Russian Literature. Columbia's program was structured in this way because Columbia was founded before the United States and began as King's College. It still has a British structure.

The course work and student teaching took five years. Jasmine was also required to take another Slavic language so she took Polish. She had added a Jewish emphasis and also took Yiddish. She was the only non-Jewish, non-Yiddish speaker and Polish Catholic in the class. This made for some interesting conversations although she did well in Yiddish class.

Jasmine was very conscientious as a teacher of Russian 1 and 2. She made sure every student in her class passed with at least a C. She said sometimes this was challenging because occasionally a student would have no aptitude for language and just would not drop the class.

Jasmine's independent thinking and teaching style would sometimes put her at odds with the teaching staff. The stress of this and the lack of family or friends and her dislike of the concrete jungle feel of New York City caused Jasmine to be depressed. She was having difficulty with her first Master's thesis but managed to complete it in two weeks when given an ultimatum. Her professors were amazed at the quality of her thesis given the short amount of time she took to complete it.

I happened to be volunteering at a place for families of child cancer patients and got into a conversation with one of the other volunteers. She happened to be a teacher in the very high school that Jasmine graduated from. I asked her if she was teaching there when Jasmine was there and if she remembered Jasmine Garcia. She said "oh her, she was terrible" and she went on and on about what a problem Jasmine was in the school. I smiled and asked her if she wanted to know what Jasmine was doing now. She said yes. I told her Jasmine graduated college and was awarded five out of six full fellowships for a Ph.D. in Russian Literature. She chose to attend

Columbia University and was in the graduate program at that time. The teacher was dumbfounded and asked me if Jasmine's former principal knew this. I told her I did not believe that she did.

Jasmine was wise enough to know to get help with the issues that were keeping her from accomplishing her goals. Since she was on scholarship her health care was provided by the Medical Center at Columbia University and she had access to some of the best psychiatrists in the world. She was able to get going again and completed her second Master's degree.

After she had been in her apartment for four years, two two-year leases, she had only one more year at Columbia. She opted to rent a room with a woman who had been a student in the past at Barnard, Columbia's women's college, who had advertised a room for rent. It was actually part of a room with access to the kitchen and bathroom. The apartment building was close to Central Park in Harlem. Yes that Harlem.

I and Jasmine's friend Dolores helped her move to the new room. Jasmine had to recycle most of her furniture and the rest we wrestled up in the small elevator or up the narrow staircase. We also stacked 30 boxes of books in her old apartment lobby to be picked up by the Postal Service to be returned to my home. Jasmine had many boxes of books mailed from Russia to our home since Russian language books were so cheap there. Most were still on shelves or in boxes in my basement. If Jasmine needed a book she did not have with her she would call me, tell me where to find the book she needed and describe what the letters looked like in Cyrillic so I could identify it and send it to her. This she did on a regular basis hence the 30 boxes of books needing to be returned home.

After we got Jasmine settled into her new apartment, it was later than we had planned so Dolores then took the bus home and I drove first to Illinois and stayed for a few more months with my Mom whose health had taken a turn for the worse. I had Jasmine's cats with me and all the items she wanted to keep but couldn't fit in her new room. At some point Jasmine had gotten another cat, an orange tabby she named Lavrente. She got Lavrente from a foster cat home in Queens. Valera and Lavrente bonded right away. She could not keep the cats in the rented room. The cats were in two carriers stacked on top of each other in the front seat and the rest of the car was completely full which was why Dolores had to take the bus home. I was bone tired after spending the past few days cleaning and moving furniture and stayed the night in a hotel with the cats. We stopped again the next night because I couldn't keep my eyes opened. The cats sat on the window sill looking out the motel window with only their tails showing. Somehow I managed to lose Jasmine's blue Kitchenaid mixer on the trip back home.

This was the first time Jasmine was around primarily black people. She was at first taken aback by the way the black people congregated on porches and talked loudly. Then she realized this was their normal way of being. As always she fit right in.

Jasmine successfully completed her fifth and final year at Columbia taking classes and teaching. She had learned from others in the Russian Literature Ph.D. program that some people had gotten permission to return home to work on their dissertations. Jasmine asked for permission to work from home as well.

Once again I was returning to New York to help Jasmine make the move back home. I took the red eye to New York. I had a folding hand truck dolly and a bike rack in my suitcase and little else. For a few days I slept on the couch in the apartment Jasmine shared while we packed up and got the shared room back to its original condition. Jasmine had already managed on her own to wrestle the furniture she wanted to leave down the elevator or staircase. So all that was left was packing the many remaining books, taking Jasmine's art works off the walls and getting the walls back into their original shape.

This was challenging in that New York apartments have many kinds of wall surfaces since they have been remodeled so often. The walls could be plaster, wall board, or brick. I got a large container of pink spackle to cover the holes in the walls and ventured out to the Home Depot with a paint chip to get a paint match for the bright orange paint that was on the walls in her room. It was a success, the room looked exactly as it did when Jasmine moved in and she was able to get her damage deposit back.

Jasmine rented a Chrysler Town and Country that had fold in the floor second and third row seats so the entire back of the van was available for the remaining items Jasmine was taking home. We hauled four large boxes to the post office with the hand truck dolly to send home book rate. We also had to stop at Jasmine's office at Columbia University to get the art works Jasmine had there.

Jasmine had always had an interest in art. When she was younger she liked Thomas Kinkade's paintings and we had at home two of his limited edition prints. Kinkade fell out of favor with Jasmine when he started licensing his works on everything from coasters to calendars. She said it made her investment less valuable.

Jasmine became interested in Peruvian retablos and textile art and other folk art works. She said these would retain value and increase in value because they were unique works of art and also much less expensive.

I was driving and had the green light for the ramp to the George Washington Bridge when a bicyclist crossed right in front of the van. I slammed on the brake; fortunately the bicyclist passed in front of us unscathed and nothing in the back of the van broke. I always drove in the cities and Jasmine drove in the open areas. We stayed again with my Mom in Illinois halfway home.

Jasmine's experiences with men had not worked out for her and she told me she was holding in her mind the type of man she would like to have a relationship with while she was studying and teaching at Columbia. She did not go into detail about it.

During her last year at Columbia she received a Facebook friend request from a young man, Charlie, who she remembered from high school. She accepted the request and they started communicating by phone and on Facebook. As it happened he had a crush on Jasmine in high school but didn't say anything to her. They hit it off and he visited her in New York and she visited him in Colorado.

After Jasmine's return from Columbia, Jasmine and Charlie took me to dinner at The Fort, a very nice restaurant in the foothills. They wanted to live together and wanted to know if I was okay with that.

As I said Charlie was a former classmate of Jasmine's. Both were IB dropouts. Charlie went on to become a software developer and made a good income. They were coming together after life experiences had forged them into the people they were and they were happy and compatible with each other.

So Jasmine went to live with Charlie with my blessing. They had three different apartments and then came to live with me for 18 months while they saved money for a home of their own.

I gained new paint and carpet in the basement and new appliances. Jasmine and I went through all the boxes stored in the basement and they paid for two truckloads of 1-800-GOT-JUNK. They lived their own lives and the majority of the time I learned about what was going on with them from Facebook even though they were living in the same house.

Along the way Jasmine and Charlie acquired two new Bengal cats, Lord Tiberius called Lord Tibby or Tibbers (a brown Bengal) and Stormaggedon called Stormy (a silver Bengal). My Serenity and Lara, the orange tabby Jasmine found for me as a friend for Serenity at a friend of a friend's the first summer she came home, had to stay in my room. Jasmine's cats (all males) were too energetic for my girls.

I was present on one occasion though. Charlie's niece was in town and she and Jasmine were discussing being children of single parents, since Charlie's sister was married off and on and was single at that time. The topic was feeling neglected by one's mother. I heard Jasmine say that she never felt neglected by me when she was growing up. I was very moved by this because I was going to school and working five jobs at one point and sixty hours a week another time until Jasmine was six years old and the only time we had together was in the car on the way to and from babysitters. I worked very hard to complete my education by the time Jasmine was six so I could support her in her school and other activities. When I was with Jasmine I was totally focused on her and it is the quality of the time spent not the quantity.

Charlie and Jasmine purchased a home of their own with enough rooms for an office for Charlie, an office for Jasmine and a guest room.

Jasmine was working on her dissertation for Columbia, The Literary Fairytale in 19th Century Russia, because she was still on fellowship and this was her job. Jasmine said it takes a lot longer to get a Ph.D. in Russian literature than it would in math for instance because it involves reading a lot of literature which takes time.

Jasmine's Valera developed congestive heart failure. He survived nearly two years having to take medication every day. After Valera passed away Jasmine and Charlie were getting a replacement laser pointer for the cats and found a little tabby kitten with a "catality" almost identical to Valera. So they came home with Maximus Valerus or "Max." Jasmine had ordered a snow Bengal but the breeder was having difficulty coming up with a cat so Jasmine acquired an available snow Bengal she named Draco. Now I have five grand cats.

I know when I die my urn will be on a mantle or shelf somewhere in Jasmine's house with a collection of containers with the ashes of her cats. She already has Mara's and Valera's ashes.

Jasmine completed her dissertation and successfully defended it. She will "walk" (attend commencement) in May, 2016, even though she is already Dr. Jasmine Garcia. I will be there.

Since Jasmine is no longer employed by Columbia she has had a few jobs. She was in customer service at a large cable company for a month while at the same time driving for Uber. She realized that she was making as much driving for Uber part time as she was earning at the other job full time so she decided to drive for Uber and quit the customer service job. She said she isn't a cubicle girl although she could do the job and do it well if she had to. When Uber reduced the payments to the drivers Jasmine quit Uber around the time she and Charlie spent a month at his mother's home when she had a heart attack.

When they returned Jasmine signed up for some discounted cooking classes at Sur Le Table, a store that sells kitchen supplies and gives cooking classes. She found out the store was looking for a kitchen assistant for the cooking classes and she was encouraged to apply for the job. I was at the store with her and saw that the staff liked her and had a lot of respect for her. She got the cooking classes free as an employee and also forty percent off on purchases.

Needless to say Jasmine and Charlie have a dream kitchen with all the appliances and cookware they were able to get on discount.

People ask me what Jasmine plans to do with her Ph.D. Initially she had planned to become a professor. She said realistically she would only earn about $50,000.00 a year as a professor and it makes more sense to stay where Charlie could earn a good income. She could still be an independent scholar and do research and publish papers to present at Slavic conferences.

I am often told I should be so proud of Jasmine. I do not see her accomplishments as a reason for me to be proud. She accomplished them on her own with a little help and guidance from me. She has never been an extension or reflection of me, just an apprentice person who was entrusted to my care so that I could show her the ropes of life. This I did just as I herded turkeys to their food and barn when I was younger: by standing behind her and encouraging her to go in the direction she wanted to go. The decisions were hers, she got there on her own.

I admire the person Jasmine has become through the adversity she has endured. She is a thorough, professional and conscientious worker. She is a good and caring friend. She is a loving and accommodating daughter. At my request she played the bagpipe which she hadn't played in years for the birthday party of a friend and also for the funeral of a friend who was well known in the community but had little money. The gravesite for the man was donated and since he enjoyed the bagpipe, I asked Jasmine to play at the graveside ceremony. She was only asked to play Amazing Grace; however, at the last minute they asked her if she could play something as people walked to the gravesite. She remembered a slow air she had learned for a competition years before and played it. A local television station televised his funeral because of his impact on the community. Jasmine with her pipes, and the slow air in the background as the people walked to the gravesite, were on television on the evening news.

When my mother passed away in 2012, Jasmine drove with me to Illinois, helped with the funeral arrangements and put together a moving slide show with two of her grandmother's favorite songs playing in the background. Jasmine and I and my brother, with Jasmine's help because we do not speak Polish, sang the hymn "Serdeczna Matko" (Beloved Mother) in Polish at my mother's funeral. We realized at my uncle's funeral four months earlier that

"Serdeczna Matko" was the "song that everyone sings at funerals" that my mother had on her "songs I want at my funeral" list. Jasmine said that we would make that happen for her. Jasmine found out that old family pictures were being thrown away after one of my uncles died. She took it upon herself to visit the remaining older family members gathering living histories and acquiring all the photos and "death cards" (holy cards given to attendees at funerals) so the family would have them for posterity. She appointed herself the family historian and has been in contact with others in the family who had pictures and other items from the past. At this point in time all but one of the older generation have passed away.

All along as she was growing up and experiencing what I related in this narrative, I kept in my mind and heart the picture of the confident, independent, happy, caring little girl I knew, knowing I would see her again soon and I have. She is still and always the independent thinker. Once when she was discussing the abortion issue with a pro-life person she brought the conversation to a halt by saying "God gave people free will, who are you to take it from them?"

Jasmine has also been taking courses at the university in Boulder, mostly in art. She has had several hobbies, her latest is embroidery. She embroidered a memorial for Charlie's mother when his father passed away a few years ago. Now she is working on an embroidered veil for their wedding which will take place October 22, 2016. I will be there as well.

This is the end of my narrative about Jasmine, but it is only just the beginning – of the rest of her life.

To Jasmine, I say:

Congratulations!!

You have proven the naysayers wrong. You set your mind on the goal and persevered through challenges and adversity that would crush the spirit of anyone. You did it! You made it happen through sheer willpower.

Now there are no limits to what you could accomplish, and I know no matter where you go or what you choose to do in life you will be okay, you will succeed, you will prevail and you will do it in style.

Acknowledgements

— ❧ —

I started this narrative three years ago. I stopped. I did not know why I stopped.

Several months ago I met a new student hair stylist at the beauty school where I have my hair done, Wendy. Wendy has an adopted daughter that just started kindergarten. The teacher was making some of the same comments about Wendy's daughter that teachers were saying about Jasmine, i.e. she is not paying attention, etc.

I mentioned before that I have PTSD like reactions to any kind of notice and this has been holding me back from finishing this narrative. I am sure there are many people who will be at odds with me, with Jasmine and with any number of things I have written here.

I am writing this narrative for Wendy and her daughter, and for other mothers of daughters who are different, independent, gifted and misunderstood.

About the Author

—— ❧ ——

Nancy Nikt found out when she was 65 she is actually autistic. In spite of this Nancy was able to support herself, finish college and graduate school and successfully support herself and her intelligent, misunderstood daughter. She wrote her daughter's story to give hope to mothers of daughters like hers.

Printed in the United States
By Bookmasters